The Layla Diaries

Sonya Bartlett Skipworth

Photographic Credits: Ben Skipworth, *Inkwell Films*; Jessie Brooks Skipworth, *His and Hers*; and Sonya Bartlett Skipworth

Dedication

Dedicated to Phillip, aka G, daily proving that not all superheroes wear capes.

Introduction

Hi! My name is Layla and I've got a lot to say! It's all here in my diary, when I have time to stop and write, of course.

I live in Nashville, Tennessee with my mom and dad. My pretty mommy is something called a wedding picture maker. My handsome daddy does something with a different kind of camera thingy. Sometimes he says things like, "Sorry little girl, I can't play right now. I have to edit." That is not a glad thing for Layla.

My mom has her own mom and dad and they are my Nana and Pa. My mom's grandmother, Nanny, lives with Nana and Pa on a big grassy place by The Bathtub That Goes For Miles and Miles.

My dad has a mom and dad too. When I go to Alabama, I stay with them. Grammy and G are their names. They take care of me when my mom and dad do Exciting Things That Don't Include Layla. I don't mind because I love the happy place of Grammy and G's.

January 9, 2014

Dear Diary:

Hi! It's me Layla. I'm going to be staying with Grammy and G while my parents are in Gatlinburg. Why would they not want to take me? I am so much fun! I'm already starting my morning off right. I'm going to be more careful than when I was here before . . .

On my last visit to Grammy and G's I got into Aunt Sarah's aspirin and opened the bottle. It made a funny shaking noise. The little brown circles whacked each other and said, "Bonk! Bonk! Bonk!" Grammy came over with her huge eyes. She grabbed me up and kept saying, "Drop it, Layla!"

I dropped it. "Don't have a cow, Grammy!" She grabbed the bottle and got out that phone thingy and called some lady named Mrs. Poison Control. Then she called Aunt Missy. Aunt Missy told her Mrs. Poison Control was right.

I wondered, "What is she right about?" Grammy was a shaky mess. She kept giving me spoons of bubbly stuff from a brown bottle. It was gross.

Then me and my Grammy sat on the back porch. I put my head in her lap while she cried big tears and kept saying “Help me Jesus.” She called Aunt Missy again on the phone thingy and then gave me a few more spoons of the bubbly brown bottle.

My tummy was doing a little summersault inside. I started feeling a little wobbly. “Yerp . . . yerp . . .” Whew, I felt better. Grammy was very interested in my yerp for some reason. She was shaking her head and said, “I didn’t find any pills.” Silly Grammy, why would she think I would eat them? The outside is sweet but the inside, “Yuck!”

Goodbye for now, Diary!

Love, Layla

When my dad is going on a work trip and is not taking me, I lay on his suitcase real hard so he can't put his takeaway things inside. It never works and that is a sad thing in my heart.

January 10, 2014

Dear Diary:

Hi! It's me, Layla. I have had a very busy day. I wanted to see Cousin Maddie, but she is staying in a place called Hotel No Layla. It must be the funnest place because it has my name in it.

I kept trying to go where Cousin Maddie was taking a nap but Grammy put up something she called a barricade. I don't know what that means but it makes a funny sound if you knock it down. Grammy did her big eye look and she kept saying words like, "Oh my goodness, oh my goodness." Silly Grammy.

My G took me in the outside yard place that I love. When I am there I race myself back and forth across the yard. I have to stop and make sure G is watching me. He always does. He smiles at me and tells me I am so pretty and that I am good girl.

Tonight I am excited because I am sleeping on the couch in Grammy and G's room. Cousin Maddie said it was ok because she is sleeping on something Grammy calls, "The Queen's bed." Doesn't look so fancy to me. I have two blankets and a pillow so I feel like a Princess!

Bye for now, Diary!

Love, Princess Layla

This is me and my G! I love him the most. He is the best chaser ever.

February 9, 2014

Dear Diary—

Hi! It's me, Layla! Last night we had a birthday party for my dad at my Nana's house. I poked my cousin, McLovin in the eye. I didn't mean to, I was just playing with him. He gets a little cranky when there is a lot of company at one time because Nana said he gets what's called "nervous." But me, I like a lot of people—the more the better. It is just more people to play with and say, "Layla you are so pretty," or "Layla, you are a good girl."

When Grammy and G were leaving they were hugging me goodbye and my dad said, "Layla, do you want to go home with them?" He was only joking but I was looking excited with my happiest face ever so he would let me go. I sat in Grammy's lap on the way home. She squeezed me tight the whole time and said she missed me. Grammy has a nice lap. I like it.

When we got home, Uncle Matt chased me around the couch. He is fun because he plays with me and lets me show all the tricks I can do. Then he says, "Good girl, Layla." Aunt Sarah did not know I was coming so she was extra excited to see me again. I don't blame her, I am pretty fun, humbly speaking, of course. My cousin Maddie had to take a bath, and she was what Aunt Sarah called, "ticked." I don't know what that means but

I hate baths too so "ticked" must be another word for "Layla hates baths."

This morning I was ready to get going early since I have to make the most of my time. My G was leaving early. He gets up when it is still dark and goes to be a police chaplain. When people cross over the Rainbow Bridge he talks to their family so they won't be sad. I love him for that.

Grammy said, "Layla, do you need to go out?" I told her, "Yes please." She said, "Wait a minute, Layla, I have to put on a coat." "Silly Grammy," I laughed, "I don't need a coat, I already have one on!"

After I did my doodle outside I came back in and shook the wet off. Then I did a little "synchronized swimming" on Grammy's rug. When I got tired of that I got out all the toys in my basket because they are brand new to me. I haven't seen them in three weeks.

I found a bread tie on the kitchen floor and ignored all my nice toys and chewed on it until Grammy caught me and took it away. That lady may not be fast chasing me, but she's always fast at noticing anything out of the ordinary. She's worried about whatever I am chewing on. If that Grammy says, "Drop it Layla," then I drop it!

Goodbye for now, Diary!

Love, Layla

This is me with my mom and dad at my "Yay Layla Obeyed and Got to Wear a Funny Hat Class." They were very proud of me and so I smiled a good cheesy smile for my picture.

March 13, 2014

Good Morning Diary!

It's me, Layla! My Daddy was out of town working in Miami and I started feeling really bad. My poor Mommy was not sure what was wrong with me. Since she doesn't speak Layla talk and I don't speak Mommy talk I could not tell her.

She took me to my doctor and told me in the car that "They will help me get better." I'm not so sure about her words to me. That place gives me the willies! The last time I was there I ended up with a space helmet and a sore belly. "No, Mommy, I'm thinking this place is no good for Layla!"

They poked me with something sharp and then wrapped my arm up with pretty cloth with blue stars on it. They told Mommy they would call with results. I hope "results" are not sharp things. My Mommy had to take off work already so Aunt Sarah told her I could come to Alabama and stay with her and my Grammy and G! G is my favorite of course. (No offense Grammy and Aunt Sarah.)

We met Grammy halfway from Nashville and as soon as I heard I was going to her house I started crying "Hurry up Mommy!" over and over again. I kept asking, "Are we there yet?" Then, I saw her! It was my Grammy! She kept hugging me and saying, "Bless her." She says that a lot. Anyway, she put me in her car and we took off to her house. I looked out the window for a while and then I got bored so Grammy let me lay my head in her lap.

When we got to Grammy and G's, Aunt Sarah was waiting outside to get me. She took me inside and I was glad. She likes me.

I heard Grammy and Aunt Sarah talking about something called, "her medicine." I hope that is a place like the dog park. I like the dog park. Grammy went to the big white box and got out a little cup and a spoon. She said, "Layla, do you want some ice cream?" She said it in a happy sound so I'm hoping this is not like a sharp thingy.

I'm thinking, "OK Grammy, I will give this ice cream a try but, please, don't let it be sharp!" She gave me a big spoon of it and I liked it! A lot! She told me I was a good girl. I like to hear that, of course. So now anytime she goes to the big box and says, "Layla, do you want some ice cream?" I am always very happy because it tastes so good. I'm not going to tell Grammy I know she is tricking me with my medicine. That way, she will keep giving me ice cream!

Bye for now Diary!

Love, Layla

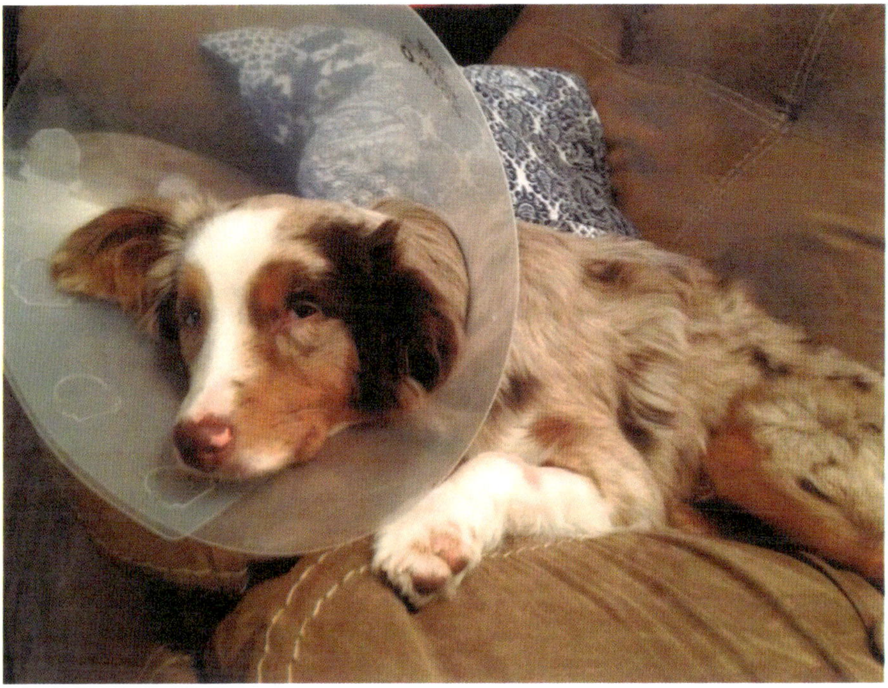

This is me when I was wearing my space helmet after my tummy surgery. As you can see I do not feel so well in my body.

March 14, 2014

Good Morning Diary!

It's me, Layla! Grammy wrapped me in a blanket last night and said I looked like a burrito. I don't know what it is but it is a funny sounding word. Burrito, burrito, burrito! When I woke up this morning I was so happy because I found myself still at Grammy and G's house! Yay! I am feeling much better today and I am so very glad.

Yesterday was a very happy day because Grammy opened the big door and let me and my Cousin Maddie look out the glass. The sun was shining and I was plotting how to get out there and run, run, run in the grass into the big world.

Maddie and I had to protect Grammy from cats and squirrels. We kept a watch and barked every time so she would know we were still on patrol. After about two hours of that I started to get bored. For some reason when I get bored I mostly hear, "No Layla."

I started boxing Cousin Maddie on the ear and she did that unhappy snapping face. I do not like that unhappy snapping face. She is not as big as I am but she is really scary when she doesn't want to play. I did what was called, "learned my lesson." But, I will probably forget my lesson in a little while and try again.

Sometimes Cousin Maddie is really cranky. Grammy says Maddie is elderly. If elderly means just sleeping, eating, and watching everybody else run and play, I'm not having any elderly, no way!

This morning Grammy gave me my ice cream and then put some water in my pink bowl. After I drank all my water I played with my bowl. I have a whole basket of toys. My Nana bought me a squeaky man that I like to play with because it makes a funny sound. My Mommy and Daddy have bought me a lot of toys too. But Grammy laughed at me because I had more fun playing with a plastic bowl. She made a movie of me and sent it to my Mommy and Daddy. I'm sure they are only drying their tears today because they must miss me so much.

I think I will rest for a little while now. I will probably need to conserve my energy because G said he would play with me when he gets home! He's WAY more fun than my pink bowl!

Bye for now Diary!

Love, Layla

This is me wrapped up in my burrito blanket!

Me and my cousin, Maddie, are sniffing out trouble!
We make a great team!

March 15, 2014

Good Morning Diary!

Hi! It's me, Layla! Happy day, happy day! When I woke up I was still at the happy place of Grammy and G's house. I went to Grammy's bed and patted her leg and quietly screamed, "Grammy get up and let us together go and wake up the sunshine!" She smiled at me and got up and followed me to the door. But there was one huge problem.

When I turned around it was NOT Grammy but a monster!!! It had Grammy's face and her sound coming from the mouth part but it was NOT my Grammy! Then the monster became Grammy again. She said, "Oh Layla, I am sorry. It's my raincoat isn't it?" Grammy totally forgot I had a thing about hoods. It makes me really quivery feeling around my insides and I just don't like them.

Then came the next huge problem. I started doing the "potty dance." But water was falling from the sky and since I'm not going near the Hooded Monster Fake Not My Grammy I was not sure what to do. She smiled and said, "It's OK Layla." Grammy got a tent on a pole and took me outside. She held the tent on a pole over me so I would not get wet. She called it an umbrella. Whatever. Just as long as it keeps my coat dry it's fine to call it anything you want oh my Real Grammy That is Not The Hooded Monster Fake Not My Grammy.

I think I will just sit here at the big glass door and watch the water drip from the sky and be glad I have this nice little rug to stretch out on. I'm going to protect Grammy from cats and squirrels again today.

After my patrol I have a very busy day lined up. Then, tonight I get to see my Mommy and Daddy. I am very excited about that because I have missed them. I have only got to see them in a small size on Grammy's talking box. But tonight I will get to see them in a big size and I am glad of that happy thing to do.

Well, now I am going to help Grammy type on the computer. She needs me to be her assistant. I like to sit beside her and pat her arm while she works. I know she is glad to have me lend a hand, uh, paw.

Bye for now Diary!

Love, Layla

I don't really like the days when the sky throws water on me. I like sunshiny ones better. Then I can wear my eye covers. I feel fancy in them so I decided to give my mom a Layla is a Supermodel Look.

May 5, 2014

Good Morning Diary!

Hi! It's me, Layla! On Saturday, I got to come to the happy place of Grammy and G's. My parents had to make pictures at a wedding so I got to stay ALL day which was a glad thing for me.

I invented a few new games. I played Layla Stays Directly Under Grammy's Feet to Check Her Extreme Lack of Coordination. Bless her. Grammy is not too steady.

I got tired of that after a while and made up the best game ever. I named it, Layla Throws Out All Her Toys from Her Basket to See How Many Times Grammy Will Pick Them Up. That was only fun for a little while because Grammy gave up WAY too quickly. Time for a new game! I played Layla Lays Down on Grammy's Shoe and Takes a Ten Minute Nap Making Grammy Afraid to Move. Grammy doesn't sit still much so I have to take advantage of it when I can.

Later on G chased me around the couch in a game called Layla Gets Chased Around the Couch by Her G. G is fast. He's way faster than poor Grammy. But Layla, is faster than both of them!

Cousin Maddie let me sit beside her on the big couch in Grammy's room. Last time I was here I played the game called Layla Steals the

Blanket from Cousin Maddie in an Effort to Get Her to Play. It was not a success but that's ok. At least she did not do that snappy cranky growly sound. She just breathed a heavy breath and put her head on the pillow.

This morning I got up before anybody else and played a game called, Layla is an Alarm Clock. Grammy smiled and patted me on the head. She made me some breakfast. Now it's time to play. I think I will invent another new game . . . .

That's all for now Diary!

Love, Layla

I try to stay right under Grammy's feet whenever possible because that lady needs a lot of help. And I mean a lot!

May 7, 2014

Good Evening Diary!

It's me, Layla! What an exciting day it has been at that happy place of Grammy and G's! When I got up this morning I had no idea how this day would turn out!

Grammy started getting ready this morning and it made me sad because I knew that meant she was going to be leaving. She was going to go to school. The only part I like about that is because when she gets home she smells like paint and crayons and little kids.

Grammy put me in the kitchen and shut the door. I started saying, "No, Grammy! NO! Layla is supposed to be on the Grammy side of the door, not on the un-Grammy side of the door!" She would not listen. I cried with my broken up heart.

Finally she came back and said, "Let's go, Layla!" with a happy Grammy face. "Let's go? Yes Grammy! Let's go! Let's Go! Let's Go! Wait! Where are we going? I don't want to go to the place with ouchy sharpy thingies."

Grammy put on my nice harness. I like it because when I get a little too excited outside and try to run far it doesn't squeeze my neck and make me gag, "Aaaaakk, Aaak, Layla is choking." Bad idea.

We got in Grammy's car and I looked out the window for a while and then we drove up to a big place with lots of wiggly kids. I wanted to smell all of them but Grammy made me sit still while she walked in the middle of the wiggly kids. Then I saw him! My Aaron! It was my Aaron!

He got in the car and I jumped in his lap and squished him with all my pounds. Boy, was he happy to see me! We drove and drove and finally we were at the surprise place Grammy promised to take me. It was Aunt Sarah and Uncle Matt's new house!

Grammy took me in the back yard and unhooked my leash. I ran and I ran and I ran! I loved the wind in my fur. I chased Aaron around and around the yard. He is fast to just have two legs. He's WAY faster than Grammy! But I'm WAY faster than him!

Later, Grammy took me to the store and bought a ginormous bag of food for me. Silly Grammy, I can't eat all that. I'm not that hungry. Bless her. She means well. The girl that worked there said I was pretty and wanted to pet me. Everybody always wants to pet Layla!

I am very tired from my exciting day. I may even sleep in tomorrow morning. I think I will set my alarm clock for 5:30. That should be good wake up time for everybody. . .

Good Night Diary!

Love, Layla

This is me and my Aaron. He is very fast to only have two legs!

May 9, 2014

Good Morning Diary!

It's me, Layla! I am still at that happy place of Grammy and G's. My dad is globetrotting and my mom has a new job so I get to play, play, play, all day, day, daaaaaayyyy!!!!

Yesterday Grammy gave me a new bowl. It was like my pink one except it was orange. I played with it until it got stuck under the couch. I used to fit under Grammy's couch but now I'm a big girl and can't do it anymore.

The first time I came to meet my Grammy and G, I also met my cousin Maddie. I was way smaller than her. The next time I came we were the same size. Then the next time I came I was way bigger than her! I wonder what made her shrink down so little?

Now that I am so tall, I can stand up on my back legs and put my chin on the table. This works really well when I give that Sad Layla Wants Something Wonderful off Your Plate Face. It doesn't work though. They said I can't have people food. I don't know why not because I is a people.

Yesterday Grammy had something sitting on the hot box. I could smell its wonderful goodness.

She walked out of the room and I decided to take a closer look.

I stood up on my back legs and there it was! Chicken! Grammy is always dropping stuff on the floor when she is cooking so I have had chicken before. But I had never seen the little green trees. I investigated them further, sniffing them. I began to inch closer. Closer. Closer. "Layla!" said Grammy. "Busted," said Layla.

I must make a mental note to be a little faster next time. Eat first, ask questions later!

Bye for now, Diary!

Love, Layla

This is me the first time I met my cousin, Maddie. I was afraid she would not like me so I stayed really close to my mom.

May 10, 2014

Good Evening Diary!

Hi! It's me, Layla! I have been missing my Mom and Dad. I was really excited about seeing them soon. I have had fun at Grammy and G's, well, until The Bad Thing That Happened Which Made Me Not So Happy Layla.

Grammy took me into the bathroom and was talking all Sweet Grammy to me. Then The Bad Thing That Happened Which Made Me Not So Happy Layla happened. Grammy was abducted by an alien! The Alien Grammy had Sweet Grammy's voice but my Real Grammy would never make me take a bath.

The Alien Grammy tried to pick me up so I made myself really low to the ground. I spraddled my legs wide, wide, wide so the Alien Grammy could not pick me up. I cried and said, "Oh Alien Grammy, tell Sweet Grammy I did not mean to drop a humongous stinky doodle in her sewing room floor. Oh, and the little yellow dribble was not what I intended either. Oh please Alien Grammy! Do not make me take a . . . ." Finally the Alien Grammy wrestled me into the tub. Did I mention I do NOT like the Alien Grammy?

The Alien Grammy started pouring water on me. I got a really quivery feeling all over and I tried to hold myself from shaking but I could not stop. The Alien Grammy kept talking in the Sweet Grammy's voice but I knew her scoundrel-ly tricks!

When it was all over, the Alien Grammy picked me up and finally put me on the good side of the tub—the outside! She got a loud blowing thingy and tried to put air on me. I was too fast for her! I ran away and shook, shook, shook, all over the Alien Grammy to melt it and it worked! The Sweet Grammy was back and she wanted to play a game of Chase Wet Layla. I liked that game and I like Sweet Grammy way better than Alien Bath Grammy!

That's all for now, Good Night Diary!

Love, Layla

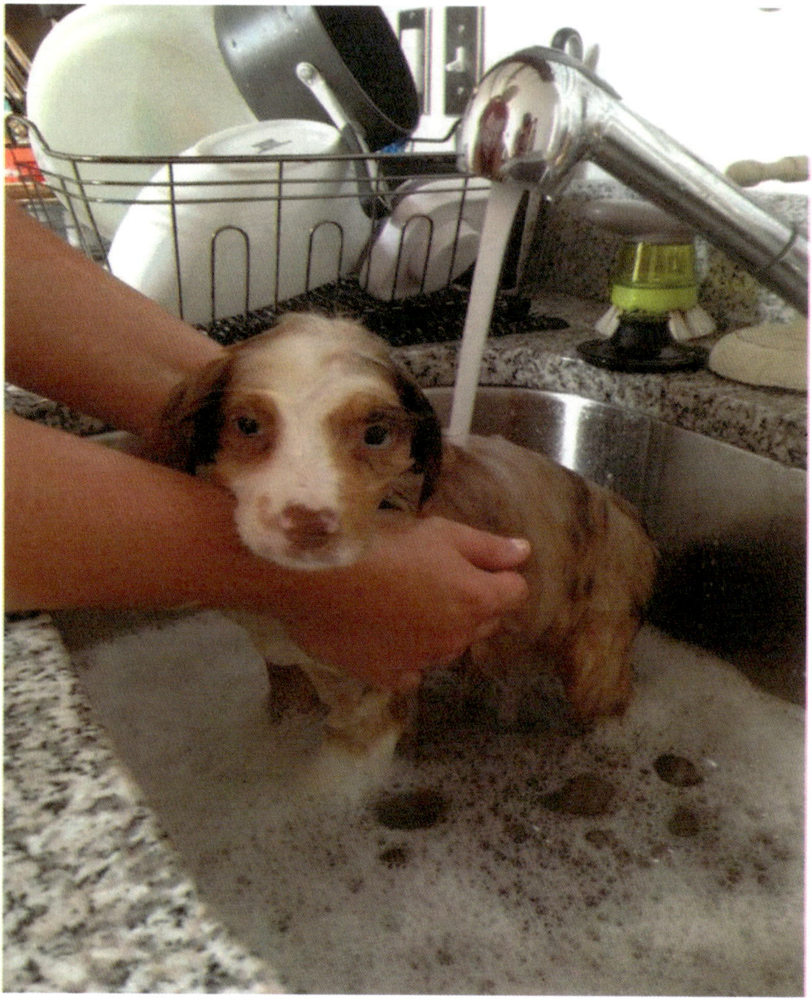

Here is me when I took my first bath. I still don't like them. I think the face I am showing says what I feel in my heart.

June 6, 2014

Hi Diary!

It's me, Layla! Today I got to come to the happy place of Grammy and G's. Grammy bought me six new bowls and my daddy played with me and my new bowls before he had to go away.

My Mom and Dad left me at Grammy and G's so I could take care of my Grammy. She is just pitiful and needs all kind of help. I wonder to myself, "Myself, how does Grammy make it when Layla is not here to take care of her?"

There was a bad crackling sound in the sky and the air was dark and windery. My Grammy was sitting in her chair and I jumped on her and mashed her so the crackling sky and waters would not hurt her. I watched her as long as I could and then my little eyelids started sinking lower and lower.

My Grammy let me watch her until I woke up. She's good that way. Then she went out in the game room and got on the Sitting Still Wheely Thing. I barked and barked and said, "Grammy get away from the Sitting Still Wheely Thing! It might hurt you." My G came in and I tried to tell him and he wouldn't listen either. He took me in the living room with him but I stayed by the door in case the Sitting Still Wheely Thing knocked

Grammy down. She might need me to help her. Poor Grammy.

She sat down and starting moving the heavy sticks back and forth. They must be really heavy because Grammy was all wheezy like I get when my necklace is too tight! My Grammy was breathing heavy. She said, “It’s OK Layla. I’m just working out.” More like passing out my dear Grammy. I cried again and said, “Grammy you are in such danger. I’ve got to take care of you!” She just smiled and patted my head. Poor Grammy. She does not know all the things lurking around that want to get her. That’s why she needs me.

G cooked supper. Everybody says I’m spoiled, but I’m thinking G spoils Grammy a little too. I sat at the table and cried a little smallish kind of sound. Grammy smiled. I was thinking Grammy would surely know that was not a Please Look at Me Adoringly sound but a Hey Give Me Something Yummy From Off Your Plate sound.

My Dad told Grammy she could not give me anything because my dad said no to that happy thing. But my daddy is not here. I inched closer and got by Grammy and she kept on eating. I stood up and announced myself real big that I was here for dinner. I laid my paw on her and looked my Layla is Starving Face.

Grammy reached on her plate and handed me a . . . bean. A bean? Grammy, give me a break–this is entirely too much cuteness for just a bean. I was hoping for a piece of your pork chop! I'll have to try harder tomorrow.

Good Night Diary!

Love, Still Hungry Layla

I've been practicing my skills for a long time. This is me the first time I went out for a stroll with my mom and dad. I cuted them into picking me up with my sad looking face.

June 7, 2014

Good Evening Diary!

Hi! It's me, Layla! Today was a fun day at the happy place of Grammy and G's. I played with my pink bowl for a while but mostly I stayed under Grammy's feet so I could be real close to her in the case of if she needed my help.

I figured Grammy was bored so I let her play Chase Layla Around the Couch Until Grammy has to Stop and Wheeze. I grabbed my pink bowl and started running all around the room darting in and out of the chairs and couches. I got up on the arm of the chair and shouted out loud, "Come and get me Oh My Wheezy Grammy Who is Morbidly Out of Shape!"

Grammy tried to talk like me. My eyes got big and I talked back, then she talked like me again. It made me feel all smiley inside my heart. She said she couldn't do it anymore because it made her throat hurt. Poor Grammy, she's falling apart. I liked to play with G better than Grammy because G does not wheeze when we chase each other. Grammy is a way better watcher than a chaser.

Tonight G took me outside. I was excited because I love the outside place but not today. It is still windery and boomy. I needed to, uh, well, you know, but I wasn't going to get off the step. I wasn't letting my G get blown away so I didn't budge myself until he gave up and took me inside.

The danger was gone but I still needed to, uh, well, you know. I couldn't wait any longer. I went to Aunt Sarah's room and dropped a doodle. But it was OK. I did it right in the doorway so she would be sure and see it. I like to be helpful and make things convenient. Tomorrow I think I will try to find even more ways to help out. I'm just good that way!

Goodnight Diary!

Love, Helpful Layla

Here is me and my dad when he had to clean up one of my doodles. He made gaggedy sounds. My mom says he is a Drama Queen.

June 14, 2014

Good Morning Diary!

Hi! It's me, Layla! Yesterday I got to find myself at the happy place of Grammy and G's house. They were so very glad to see me. My G was going to go somewhere with my dad so I decided to stay with Grammy.

In a little while the door knockded loudly and it made my cousin Maddie bark so I had to help her alert Grammy. She made me stay on the un-Grammy side of the door. That was not a good thing so I cried so she would know that she needed to hurry and come back on the Layla side of the door.

When she came on the Layla side of the door there was some more peopleses like Grammy with her. They smelled like I knowed them from somewhere. They had two tiny peopleses with them. The mommy was holding a baby little people. The mommy had a pretty mommy face. I ran over in a fast way and barked really loud, "Hello baby little people!! I have a pretty mommy too!! She smells really good. So does your mom! But your dad, I'm not sure about him.

The baby little people cried. "No baby little people! No crying! I was saying hello real nice.

That is not a good sound for Layla's ears." The baby people stopped and I was glad.

There was a girl little people with golden hair. She had dancing eyes that made me feel wiggly in my heart. She rubbed my coat and said, "Awww. She is so pretty." Then with an excited talk she said, "She's wearing a little bow! Look at her little bow! Awww she is so pretty!" I get that a lot.

Grammy put the girl little people in the big chair. She got out some good smelling things and let the little girl spoon things in and roll them up. The baby little people watched and played with the wrapper. I stood up at the counter to see if they needed my help in any way, like to eat leftovers.

When they got their food from the hot box, Grammy accidently dropped a piece for me. She's good that way. The baby little people didn't drop any of his on the floor. At all. So I decided I should stand up on my back leggies and see why no one was dropping anything by accident on purpose for Layla. Fortunately for me, I could reach the baby little people's crumbs. Thank you baby little people.

After supper Grammy gave the baby little people a bath in the kitchen sink. It made me nervous because I am not a fan of the bath tub. The baby little people splashed water everywhere and the girl little people helped with the soap.

Then Grammy took the baby little people and the girl little people down to the big bathroom. I started pacing because I knew that poor girl little people was going to have to get into that tub. I waited at the door and never moved because I knew she might need me and I wanted to stay close in case she needed rescuing from the Tub That Layla Hates.

When they finished and everybody was smelling in a fresh clean way Grammy sat on the couch with them and gave the baby little people a bottle while the girl little people watched something with little kids on it. I patiently let the baby little people drink his bottle until I could not wait any more.

I eased myself up close to Grammy's face and gave her the stare down. I was giving her the silent glare of OK Grammy Layla Time I am Tired of Being Patient Play with Me Look. I reached out with my paw and kept patting her and not so subtly saying with my eyes, "OK, My Oblivious Grammy Who is Ignoring Layla, I've had enough of this game called Let's Ignore Layla." She patted my head and told the girl little people we were going to play a game with Layla. I was so happy that I wagged my nub in an excited way.

She sat the girl little people up high, just in case. She held the baby little people and chased me around the couches. Poor Grammy is already slow anyway. The extra weight didn't help her at all. She became Oh My Wheezy Grammy really quick.

The girl little people decided she wanted to play. Who could blame her? Now, let me tell you, she is FAST. She is like greased lightning! She chased me fast and the baby little people made a squeally sound and waved his arms and legs, which made me run faster.

After playing a while I was a little glad that the girl little people wanted a game from the scary closet. They sat at the table and I laid right under her feet in the case of if she needed me. You just never know when a squirrel might come in the house.

When their daddy and pretty mommy came back they talked to Grammy and then Grammy took me outside to say goodbye. By the time my daddy and G got back I was exhausted. I laid in the floor while Grammy cooked for them and I was too tired to get up even if Grammy did drop something.

Later, Grammy wrapped me in my burrito blanket. She patted me and told me I was a sweet, good girl. I drifted off to sleep and dreamed about the girl little people and the baby little people.

Bye! That's all for now, Diary!

Love, Layla

Here I am, hard at working guarding all my peoples.

July 4, 2014

Good Morning Diary!

Hi! It's me, Layla!

Yesterday my daddy packed me in the car and said we were going to Alabama. That made my heart wiggle in an excited way! My daddy said it wouldn't be long because we were only going half-way. "Daddy do not take me to Halfway! You said we were going to Alabama and Alabama means Grammy and G's. I do not want to go to the Un-Grammy and G Place of Halfway!"

The car drove and drove for a long time until I saw my Grammy and my G. I jumped on my G over and over. I wagged my nub because I love my G the most. Grammy took me to a grassy place so I could, well, you know. Grammy is always worried about taking me out to uh, well, you know. I guess that's because she is the only one at her house who knows how to use paper towels and floor cleaner.

While the car was driving I was not glad. I could not get comfortable. I laid down a while and that was not fun. I watched the trees swoosh by. No excitement there either.

Grammy turned around and picked me up and put me in the front seat with her. Now that is a good place to sit! Right in my Grammy's lap so she can be very close to me.

The car stopped driving and my G got out and went inside a big box and the doors closed behind him. I was very concerned that he might not be able to get out of the box. I stood up on my Grammy's lap and looked out the window with all my patience. Still no G.

A lady walked out of the box. Did that box turn my G into a lady? I was one sad girl because I wanted G to hurry up. I cried in a tiny small sound. Grammy patted my back and said, "G will be out in a minute." I decided I would not even blink my little eyes just in case the box did not let G go I might be needed to save him.

Then a man came out of the box. It was not my G either. Since it was not my G, I put my eyes on mean focus and frowned at him. Finally I saw the box let my G go—and it even gave him some little bags!

When the car brought us to the happy place of Grammy and G's, the first thing I did was go to my toy basket and get my pink bowl. Ahhh . . . now Layla is a happy camper!

Bye! That's all for now, Diary!

Love, Layla

If I had only known what was going to happen to me the next day I would have stayed wrapped up in my burrito blanket and not come out. At. All.

July 5, 2014

Good Morning Diary!

Hi! It's me, Layla! I hope you're ready because I've got A LOT to say about what happened to me yesterday. The day started out at the happy place of Grammy and G's. Grammy and G were excited to tell me we were going to see my Nana and Pa. I was one glad girl!

When we got to Nana's, I was even gladder because there were three little girl peoples and a little baby people at her house! Two of the little girl peoples played chase with me in the yard. They ran fast, fast, fast, but since I have two extra legs it makes me the fastest of all!

I ran in big circles in my Nana's yard until I was tired and then I followed Grammy and G down to where Grammy's little bathtub was floating in the Huge Bathtub that Goes for Miles and Miles.

I do not like a bath anyway so I am not especially fond of the Huge Bathtub that Goes for Miles and Miles. Grammy walked out into the Huge Bathtub that Goes for Miles and Miles and I barked and said, "Uh, hello Grammy! This is not a good place for you. The bath water wet on my feet and I backed up quick fast because Layla and this place are not a good mix. No way!

Both of the little girl peoples let the Huge Bathtub that Goes for Miles and Miles wash over their little feet and I said to them ever so loudly, "Little girl peoples! No! Stay away!" But they were picking up rocks and smiling so I guess it was a happy place for them.

Grammy and G got inside the little tub that sits on top of the Huge Bathtub that Goes for Miles and Miles. I barked and barked. Grammy tried to put me in there with her and I made myself stiff so she couldn't do it. My good Uncle Tommy said, "She can stay with me." I love him for saying those words to my Grammy.

Grammy and G floated along the Huge Bathtub that Goes for Miles and Miles and I kept following them in the grass trying to tell them this was not a good idea for my Grammy and G but they just wouldn't listen.

I ran closer and closer to the side of the Huge Bathtub that Goes for Miles and Miles and whoosh—it jerked me into it and pushed me down and covered me up! Double woof Layla! It's definitely time to panic because you have just been snatched up by the Huge Bathtub that Goes for Miles and Miles!

I fought it and fought it and then my Uncle Tommy reached out into the Huge Bathtub that Goes for Miles and Miles and grabbed me out of its clutches. I stared at it with a mean frown and then ran away from it shaking its leftovers off my coat.

Well! I will not be going that close to the Huge Bathtub that Goes for Miles and Miles ever again! And I do mean EVER AGAIN! Grammy and G came back from floating on the Huge Bathtub that Goes for Miles and Miles and I was glad it did not grab them like it grabbed me!

I played some more with the little girl peoples and Grammy in Nana's back yard until it was time to go inside. The little baby people was on the floor and I went over to him and sniffed him gently and let him rub my coat. I like the baby little people because he has love in his eyes for me and even though he can't say those words I know what he means.

When it got dark all the peoples went outside and made a crowd sit. I visited a little with everyone so they could pet me and say I was a pretty girl. I went to sit in my Grammy's lap because everybody excitedly was saying words of "It's time for the fireworks!!!"

I was thinking to myself, "Fireworks! I love Fireworks! What are Fireworks?" Little did I know Fireworks was not going to be a happy thing. Not. At. All.

There was a light in the sky. The stars were falling and there was a loud boom! I started screaming to all my peoples to get up and run from this thing called Fireworks because it is going to hurt you! Fireworks are not good! Fireworks is a Sky MONSTER!!!!!!! Get up! Get away from this awful Screaming Fireworks Sky Monster!

I cried and cried until I completely broke out of my harness and kept running in circles around the house warning all of my peoples about the dangerous Screaming Fireworks Sky Monster. My Grammy, who is not fast at all, mind you, came quick flying to the front of Nana's house and shouted to me over the loud sound of the Screaming Fireworks Monster, "Come on Layla! Let's go inside!"

"Grammy," I said in my most frightened feeling, "You're the only one who understands the danger! Yes! By all means and with haste! Let's get away! Are you with me Grammy?" Grammy's legs went faster than ever and she took me inside Nana's house.

I jumped on the couch with her and tucked myself under her back and between her elbow arm. I shook like I never shook before because of the Screaming Fireworks Sky Monster. I was not coming out. Ever. And I mean ever!

My G finally came in and tried to pick me up. I made myself heavy and crammed myself further behind Grammy's elbow arm. I love my G the best but I'm not going anywhere. Ever. And I mean ever!

In just a few seconds my Uncle Hero Tommy the Lifesaving Uncle that saved me from the Huge Bathtub that Goes for Miles and Miles, came in to see about me. He patted my head and said nice words to me. One more of my people accounted for now. I'm glad the Screaming Fireworks Sky Monster did not get him too!

In a few minutes the rest of my peoples were able to escape from the Screaming Fireworks Sky Monster and I was glad because they all kept coming by and patting my head and saying, "Bless her heart." The little girl people that I love took my face in her hands and patted me.

But, Layla was still not moving! Ever. And I mean ever. Then Grammy said she was sorry she had to move but she had to go home. She said my daddy and mommy would be there soon. I wanted Grammy to sit like a rock and cover me some more.

I finally made myself soft and let G pick me up. He handed me to my Pa so he could take me upstairs and put me in the bed. I was tired and stressed and still quivery all over.

Then I said, "Good night all my peoples. I love you but I definitely don't love the 4th of July!"

That's all for now, Diary!

Love, Layla

Make no mistake about it. I did NOT LIKE the Huge Bathtub that Goes for Miles and Miles or the Screaming Fireworks Sky Monster.

August 23, 2014

Good Evening Diary!

Hi! It's me, Layla! Last night I got to sleep at my Pa, Nana, and Nanny's house. My Nanny has been sick so when I got there I wanted to go look close at her face because it is my job to take care of all of my peoples.

This morning I was upstairs with my parents in my mom's old bedroom where she lived before she was my mom. She and my dad were getting ready to go make pictures at a wedding. I heard the words of my Grammy downstairs. Her words kept saying, "Layla!" I cried for her to hear my words back, "Hello, Oh My Grammy who is on the Not Layla Side of the Door!"

Finally the door opened and I ran fast quick down the stairs to see my Grammy. I kept mashing into her legs because I know she was glad to see me. She patted me and said, "Hello, Pretty Girl." Those words from Grammy's mouth always make me glad in my heart.

She put me in her car and said more good words of, "We are going to see your G!" My G? I love my G! Yes! I was excited to see G and my cousin Maddie Who Sometimes Does the Growly Snappy Face at Me.

When we got in the house I ran straight to where cousin Maddie stays when I visit. It is called "Hotel No Layla." That is not a funny thing to me. I have become a big girl. I was just a baby then and I don't think I should be held responsible for my actions.

I shouted out to her as I ran to her little bed, "Hello Oh My Cousin Maddie that I Love who Sometimes Does that Growly Sound at Me!" She was not in her little bed. I picked up her little blanket and she wasn't under it either. I sniffed around because I think a robber must have taken my cousin Maddie. I mean, that is only reasonable.

Grammy said, "I'm sorry Layla. Maddie is not here. Aunt Sarah got married and took Maddie to her house where she and Uncle Matt live now." I wondered why Grammy was talking all crazy like that to me. Who in their right mind would want to leave the happy place of Grammy and G's? Grammy patted my head and said, "It's OK Layla. You can see Maddie another time, just not today." I just don't understand all my peoples sometimes.

I pulled back the curtain and bent back some of the mini-blinds so I could see. Grammy asked me if I was hungry and she got me something to eat. She started to walk off and I followed her. I was not letting that lady out of my sight because she might disappear like Cousin Maddie! She sat in the floor beside me. Since I knew she was not leaving, I started eating.

I picked up a few kibbles and accidently dropped them on the floor. When I finished everything in my bowl, I sniffed the kibbles and decided I didn't want to eat them off the floor. Grammy pushed them into a pile. I ignored the pile. Grammy put the Floor Kibbles into my bowl. I glared at her with mean eyes that said, "Uh, hello Grammy. You can't trick me. Those are the same exact kibbles from the floor. I did not plan to eat them so putting it in the bowl doesn't change my feelings about the Floor Kibble."

For the rest of the day I stayed really close to Grammy. Every time she moved I followed her. I mostly played the game I love of Layla Lays Right Up Next to Grammy's Feet and Watches Her While She Works and Makes Her Trip. I know Grammy wants me to stay close because she has missed me.

I guess that's all I have to say for now because I'm a tired girl. I've got to rest up for tomorrow. It is my job to keep everyone busy so I need to be ready.

Good Night Diary!

Love, Layla

My Pa lets me sit by him on the couch. He has a nice moustache. I like it very much.

September 14, 2014

Hello Diary!

It's me, Layla! I can add today to the top of the list of Layla's Worst Day, Ever. I was minding my own business. I really was, I promise. Then, Layla's Worst Day, Ever happened.

Grammy was at the kitchen table working and I was right under her feet in the case of if a squirrel came and tried to bother her. She said, "Layla, do you want me to make some sunshine for you?" She knows this is my favorite. She opened the big door for me so I could stretch out on my little rug and see into the outside place I love.

I was on patrol and warned Grammy about several invading squirrels and a few colorful birds. Then, I saw IT. IT was very interesting. IT was wriggling up under the bottom of the glass coming in from the outside place.

I said, "Well hello little wiggly crawly thing. You sure look soft. You sure look soft and yummy." But, I will tell you right now, it was NOT soft and it was NOT yummy! At. All.

Before Grammy could get to me, slurp. Down the hatch! It was even too late for "Drop it, Layla," because I had already dropped IT—into my tummy. That was when I realized it had become Layla's Worst Day, Ever.

My mouth was on fire. My throat was on fire. My tummy was on fire. I went over to Grammy's couch and kept running my tongue all down the cushions trying to scratch the IT off. IT was there, burning, and burning. Grammy grabbed something and made me chew it up. It did not help me. At. All.

I licked all over the floor trying to scrape the Burning IT off my tongue. Grammy called Aunt Missy and she told her what to do. I wish it had been that simple. It was hopeless.

Every time I went outside I snatched up grass and ate it. As soon as I got back in, my stomach said, "Hey, that stuff's not staying in here!" Yerp, out it came. Layla's Worst Day, Ever was just not a fun day. When I wasn't yerping up grass I was licking things, anything trying to get IT off my tongue.

Grammy said, "No more eating caterpillars, Layla." So *that's* what IT is called. Don't worry oh my Cautious Worry Wart Grammy, I will not ever eat another one of those again. Ever.

It's been a long day.

Good Night, Diary!

Love, Layla

This is IT. If you want a snack, this is not a good choice. Trust me on this one! Would I lie to you? Not on purpose anyway . . .

58690788R00036

Made in the USA
Lexington, KY
19 December 2016